Chapter

Mr. Ma

People often ask me where my name comes from and I usually answer - my parents

Louay Pierre Habib was born in Baghdad General Hospital on 20th September 1963, to an English mother Christine and Iraqi father, Habib, their second son after Nabile, who was born just 364 days earlier. JF Kennedy was just about to be assassinated in the USA, and there was a military coup in Baghdad, with thousands of people being shot dead. On a lighter note The car manufacturing firm Lamborghini was founded in Italy in 1963.

My mother was so convinced I was going to be a girl that she purchased an entire infant wardrobe in pink. When I came into the world, I was blessed with a full head of hair and my mother held me in her arms and called me Heidi. Obviously the first time she had to change my nappy she realised by the size of my tackle that I was in fact a boy. Unfortunately, there was no plan B on the name, so my beautiful, yet wrinkled form, was named Mr. Magoo in the interim. My parents eventually came up with Louay (meaning strong) and Pierre (after my mother's brother Peter, whom I never had the chance to meet). Habib was in fact a made up name as well. It is similar to Smith in the Western World. Our original family name was Abdul Ahad, meaning "servant of the only One". Bit of a dead ringer for a Christian Arab. We lived in Baghdad until I was about two, and left for England. My great uncle had to bribe military at the airport to let us board the plane.

My parents returned to live in Surrey, England and my father and Uncle set up one of the first American style hamburger and fried chicken restaurants in the country. Back then McDonalds was a song about an old man with a farm. My Dad and Uncle fought bitterly over the name of the restaurant and my father won, naming the Earls Court establishment Stampede. My uncle wanted to call it Kentucky Fried Chicken, because the name hadn't been registered in the UK yet. Things might have been very different if my Uncle had got his way. My father also set up one of the first high street dry cleaning shops in the world, and when my Uncle returned to Canada, they sold the restaurant business and my father concentrated on the dry cleaning.

Toronto, Canada Expo '67. Note left arm in cast. Right arm was broken shortly after its removal! Thanks for the pic Mike!

In the early days, we lived above the shop on the Kingston By Pass and we made enough money in the first week to celebrate with a fish and chip supper. My mother ran the counter, as we were just nippers, she had to look after us as well. My mother tells me we used to duck under the counter when a customer came in and play in the dirty clothes.

Through a lot of hard work, my parents business thrived reaching 18 outlets at one stage. So much so that they could just afford to send us to private school. I can remember quite a few occasions when the bills were not paid but we got by. I was fairly successful at school, nothing special, but then I discovered girls and alcohol around my 16th birthday and it all went Pete Tong. I made a right horlicks of my A-Levels and scraped into Ealing College to take a Business Studies Degree, sponsored by an commercial estate agent. I spent the next four years experimenting with all sorts of things but none of them had sod all to do with Business Studies. In the last year, I turned it round, and got lucky in the exams. I passed the degree and took a job with the commercial estate agent.

I forgot to mention that my first love was rugby, I played from the age of 8, and by the time I was 18, I had become good enough to play for Harlequins Colts. However, I got smashed to bits playing at Leicester Tigers and never really played again. I had been racing at a few Cowes Weeks with a friend from work, Andrew McLelland, and that's were the sailing all began really.

Chapter Two

Go West

In 1989, the Berlin Wall had come down and thousands of Chinese gathered in Tianaman Square demanding democracy. Maggie Thatcher's Government abolished dual tax relief on mortgages, causing a a major boom and bust in the property market, and my girlfriend wanted to get engaged, which was way too early for me. With my job going tits up and no girlfriend. I didn't have much of a handbrake on life, so I decided to take off and sail to the Caribbean. Keep in mind, I have never sailed outside the Solent before. Andrew McLelland got me a ride on a Swan 42 competing at La Nioulargue in St.Tropez. After the regatta, I ended up as delivery crew to Palma Mallorca. This is where I learnt to swear in Dutch. The weather was pretty miserable and the Dutch crew spent most of the time chucking up and hurling abuse. We had no electrics after one terrifying lightening storm, and made Mallorca by dead-reckoning.

I spent a month in Palma, polishing guard rails looking for a ride to the Caribbean. I started working on a two-masted schooner called Puritan. The first day I was sent up the rat lines to varnish the foremast with no lifeline, just a wooden bench to lower myself down on. The crew were all as mad as hatters. One day we headed up into the mountains in two Fiat bubble cars. There was a crew member sitting on the roof of each, firing mini-rockets at each other, as we drove through small Mallorcan villages, with old ladies dressed in black running for cover. We got absolutely shit faced on local wine at a place called the Rabbit Hutch in the mountains, and then drove back down to the bowling alley. Strikes were non-existent, just getting the ball in the right lane was an achievement! They called me 'lunch time' on Puritan, because that was the only pay I got, and just before the boat was about to go across the Atlantic, the Skipper told me that they don't take novices and promptly told me to push off.

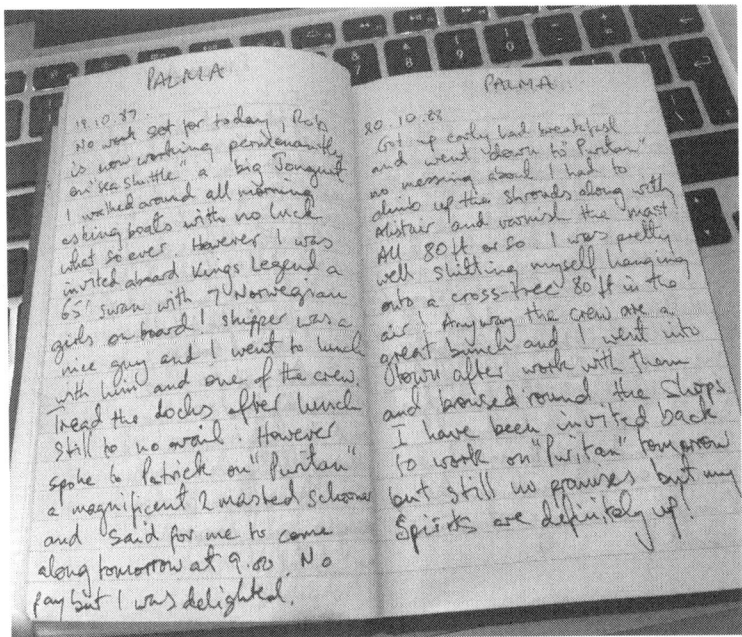

I had met a water gypsy called Rob, who had been working and living on boats for several years and we both got fired about the same time. It was Guy Fawkes Night and we decided to cheer ourselves up by taking our stuffed Guy Fawkes around the marinas, asking for 'a beer for the Guy'. We met up with another Brit, Mike Sturrock and proceeded to get drunk as lords.

Your truly sharing a moment with Rob on board Voyager

That evening we set fire to the Guy on the beach and could see police cars approaching in the distance. Now trying to explain to a Spanish Police officer, that we were celebrating the actions of a Portuguese immigrant trying to blow up the British Houses of Parliament, was going to be a bit tricky. Especially as it looked like a bunch of nutters had set fire to a real person. We did the right thing and scarpered to avoid arrest. We met up the next day and Mike, who was the skipper of a Morgan 46 Voyager, employed us as crew. We were heading for the Caribbean.

Voyager was owned by a retired British Navy Officer, Captain Brown, but he was back in the UK. First mate was a great bloke, Luiz from Brazil. The crew also had two girls, Tara from UK, and Rob's Danish girlfriend, Mette. We left Palma almost immediately, bound for Gibraltar. Voyager was a real caravan of a boat, it even had a bath. Everything worked okay but she was old and tired and needed some TLC. We got to Gibraltar, provisioned her and set off for the Canaries but a few miles out, the engine blew a gasket and we returned to Gib. A Levante blew for two weeks and nothing went anywhere, including us.

Stuck in Gibraltar with 50 knots of wind blowing chairs into the air, and a virtual river flowing down the rock, is not much fun. We passed the time playing Drivial Dispute and drinking Woods 100. We ventured out to Tarifa one day, and looked out over the Strait of Gibraltar. Oh my word, there were waves like cathedrals, Mother Nature is some force when you see it like that. Spume flying through the air, a foaming sea and the noise, the deafening shriek of the wind. One night we ventured out and there were thousands of afro-Caribbeans in town. A US Aircraft Carrier had managed to get shore parties into Gib, the place was like a war zone. We were about to go into a pub one night, and I was just about to turn the door handle, when from within I heard the sound of a chair being split over someone's back and a lot of broken glass was flying – "Let's try somewhere else." I muttered.

Eventually the Levante disintegrated and we set off towards Gran Canaria, 500 miles away in the Atlantic Ocean. There was barely a breadth of wind for five days, and we motored along side a 70-footer through glassy flat seas. The 70 footer had four Aussies chicks on board, who were mostly naked, and also a kitten which climbed the rigging. It was all a bit bizarre. We stopped everyday to have cocktails with the naked Aussies girls. Unfortunately they always dressed for sundowners! We also created a 'fuck up board'. Some writing paper on the head door, designed to leave messages when people made a mess of something. The first entry was Louay's mum 1963.

We spent a couple of days in Las Palmas provisioning and a few changes to the boat's specification, which really made the boat look like a real khazi. Drums of fuel lashed to the guard rail with a bit of old carpet to stop the deck getting rusty, and a long piece of 4x2 on the spinnaker pole to strengthen it. However, the skipper Mike, new what he was doing. He was only 21 and had already crossed the Atlantic three times in the last two years. The fuel was for the generator which supplied all of our electrical needs and increased our motoring capability by 100s of miles. The spinnaker pole, well, we never bust it, but downwind sailing without a spinnaker in a 40 ton bathtub would be bloody slow. Safety was top priority, we all had roles if we abandoned ship and a grab-bag was made up and lashed to the companion way. When we provisioned the boat, not a single piece of cardboard box came on board. Cockroaches are not a lot of fun out in the Atlantic.

Voyager had no satellite phone and very old navigational equipment. Our only real link with the outside world was an short wave radio, which produced 3000 volts through the backstay when it was transmitting, we only used it once. By Las Palmas I had now sailed about 1000 miles offshore but I don't feel ashamed to say I was bricking it when we left Las Palmas to cross 2,500 miles of Atlantic Ocean.

Chapter 3

Gimli Son of Gloin

About four days into the Atlantic crossing our fridge packed up, with all of the meat defrosting, we gorged on burgers and chicken for the next few days but after that the cuisine took a bit of a dive. However, there were a few exceptions. Luiz was the king baker, making two loaves a day shaped like 36C tits. Armed with spam, a few carrots and some onions, I have to say my Chinese stir fry was award winning. Rob was bloody hopeless, he made what can only be described as a congealed mess, dripping in what we coined sperm sauce, you had to shut your eyes to eat it. However, Rob did mange to catch a good size Dorada, which he cut into steaks and was curried..delicious.

After a few relatively easy days at sea, we had settled into our watch system. My watch was myself and Luiz; three hours on, six hours off. Rob and Mette was the watch after us, on one occasion I knocked went into their aft cabin and Rob was feasting on a fish supper..it wasn't the Dorada.

We had all decided not to use the auto-pilot, and hand steer the whole way. Luiz suggested we try two slots of 45 minutes each at the wheel and it worked very well. However, Voyager was not exactly the ideal boat for Atlantic swell. A normal Atlantic wave is about 4 metres high and 100 metres long. As the wave picked up the stern, Voyager would begin to turn sideways, so you would need to correct the steering, once you have reached the top of the wave, the bow goes down and you need to correct the steering back again. You get the rhythm of this corkscrew motion.

Mid-Atlantic Incompetence revealed by fixation with compass!

Steering is all relatively easy during the day, but as I found out at night, you can really make a mess of it. I was on the wheel at night, with Luiz rolling a smoke in the cockpit, when I began to realise that the wave that was picking us up was a rogue. About 1 in every 50 Atlantic waves is about 10 metres high, and in the darkness I didn't see it coming. As we came down the wave, the speed went through the roof, and I over corrected the steering. It was a bit like jack-knifing a lorry in a river. I was thrown off the wheel, and properly shitting myself, got back on it and straightened up Voyager, before the next wave hit us side on. It took a few minutes to get back in the groove. Mike the skipper appeared out of the hatch, he had been sleeping in the forepeak with the hatch open, and he was wetter than an otter's pocket. Luiz was pissing himself laughing. "I don't know why you think it is so funny." scowled Mike. "My bunk's bone dry because I was lying on it, yours is soaked clean through the mattress." A hint of a grin was on his lips.

The watch system allowed me to read the entire trilogy of the

Lord of the Rings. I became the dwarf warrior, Gimli son of Gloin, welding my pretend battle axe around the decks. We all go a bit crazy out in the Atlantic. Life is very different, no sofa, no TV and no contact with the outside world. The boat becomes your environment, the crew your only social side, save the occasional sighting of a ship or wildlife. We hardly saw a single boat in 23 days but wildlife was more abundant. Watching dolphins playing in the bow, or sweeping under the boat at night like glowing torpedoes is pretty awe inspiring, but to me the most impressive are the flying fish, gliding above the waves to escape Voyager's hull, believing it to be a predator.

Mike was a dab hand with a sextant and a most of us had a go at triangulating our position, we then compared it to our GPS position and most of the time we were pretty spot on. Luiz taught me about the night sky and I became a firm admirer of Orion's Belt. To this day, when I see it in the sky it makes me think of that Atlantic crossing.

Go south until the butter melts is the phrase, meaning don't try to turn west to early or you will not pick up the trade winds, and end up in the windless conversion zone of the two tropics. We went south to about the Cape Verde Islands, before turning southwest to point our bow at Barbados, 2000 miles away. Deep into the Atlantic the salinity drops so much that with a bucket or two of sea water you can wash every day. It is a blissful existence with warm air both day and night and constant breeze from the trade winds. We did get caught in a light patch nearly half way and used the opportunity to go for a swim. It is a pretty eerie feeling, knowing that you are a thousand miles from land, save the floor of the Atlantic Ocean 12000 ft below you. We cracked open our one bottle of wine and ate a cake for our halfway party. Mike decided to dress up half as a woman, which was all a bit odd! Halfway across the Atlantic, a part from Point Nemo in the Southern Ocean, it is as far away from land as you can possibly get, you are at least 7 days from a hospital or further away than an astronaut, so to speak. You are definitely on your own.

Chapter 4

Driving Home for Christmas

About ten days from Barbados, we were due to make land around Christmas Day. We hadn't brought presents, crackers and a turkey, but Mike had stowed some basic Christmas decorations, and up they went. Mette, who was now almost always topless, was our Christmas Fairy. I didn't really see too much of Tara during the trip, Mike and Tara were the watch before us and after they woke us up, Tara would usually go straight to sleep, although I did catch her reading a porn mag one morning. Tara was as I am sure still is a lovely girl and a far better sailor than me. Mike hardly ever seemed to sleep at all. He was always up, fixing something or working something out.

After over three weeks at sea, we knew we were getting close, the flying fish were growing in number and when we spotted some low cloud ahead of us, we knew that within hours we would see Barbados. The island is pretty flat, a coral atoll and it is 150 miles out into the Atlantic from the rest of the Caribbean, so it is pretty remote really. The first boat we saw was a game fishing motor boat. The guy saw our quarantine flag and was waving like mad. It was the first person other than the crew I had seen for three weeks, it was very surreal.

In those days there was no dock in Carlisle Bay, so we found a mooring buoy pumped up the dingy and went ashore. My parents had flown out to meet me, and I kid you not, the first person I saw at the dock was my mother. After a big kiss and a hug, my Dad said, "well what are you going to do next?" Have a beer I said and we found the nearest bar and got stuck into the first beer for nearly a month. All of us that is except Mike, who headed straight for a BBQ shack and ate two whole fried chickens. We had Christmas Day together at my parents hotel and then I said goodbye. Tara and Mette and Luiz were flying home, and Mike and Rob sailed Voyager to St.Lucia, to meet up with the owner. This was before the days of cell phones and facebook and it was a long time until I caught up with Luiz again, and I have never seen Mette since. I think I spotted Tara in the Pier View in Cowes about 25 years later. Mike and Rob - I was going to have a bit more fun with yet.

Chapter 5

Wacky in the Windwards

After Voyager left Barbados, I spent New Year with my folks in a five star hotel. Compared to my bunk next to Voyager's noisy engine, the room was a palace, with a balcony looking out over the ocean and chocolates on the pillow and fresh linen sheets. The huge bathroom was light years away from a bucket of salty water, and I remember turning the big gold taps off in the shower to conserve water...the habits at sea were still there. My parents suggested that I fly home with them but I wanted to experience the Caribbean, not just sail there. My time in Barbados was luxurious but I did pop down down to the seedy part of Bridgetown, playing pool for dollars with the locals, drinking Cockspur Rum and chicken roti with bones in it. I decide to fly to St.Lucia and catch up with Mike, Rob and Voyager.

The short flight to St.Lucia was my first experience of the Caribbean airline Liat. Also know as Luggage In Another Terminal or Leave Island Any Time. I paid my for my flight and was handed a boarding pass resembling a bus ticket and to be fair the flight was fine. However, over the years they have managed to screw up in more ways than you could possibly imagine. I arrived in St.Lucia and headed to Rodney Bay, where Voyager was moored. Mike had gone back to the UK but Rob was on board and we went for a beer in the A-Frame, not so much a bar as a shack with tables and chairs to drink beer in. I booked into a shit heap of a hotel in the capital Castries but it wasn't long before I moved in with Rob on Voyager. We were both pretty skint but one day we decided to do a bit of exploring and took the reggae bus from Rodney Bay in the north of the island to Marigot Bay in the south. The hour ride cost one EC Dollar about 25pence. The transit van was packed with locals, chickens and you name it. Just when I thought it couldn't take another person, the driver pulled up and picked up a mother and child. The mother squeezed her way into the seat in front of me and literally through the kid over her shoulder onto my lap. The little boy looked at the strange looking white guy with some curiosity, feeling my hair and touching my face to see if I was real. Remember this was the late 80s, and tourism had not really come to St.Lucia, and where it had, foreigners were shipped into all inclusive compounds.

We got off the bus and admired the Pitons, the two volcanic mounds are about 2,500 ft high rising above the stunning Marigot Bay. It is where the 1967 film Doctor Dolittle was shot starring Rex Harrison, and a baby elephant called Eric, who was apparently allergic to peanuts. I nearly jumped out of my skin when we saw an elephant on the beach. Apparently the film makers just left him there after the film. He was quite harmless but being the only elephant on the island must have made him a bit mad. In those days there was no guided tours or hotels in the south of St.Lucia but we were intrigued by a sign on the side of the road, scrawled on the wooden plank was – Trespass on my land 3 dollar. So we did.

We were met by a young man, who started off being quite aggressive but when we pulled the coins out he calmed down and led us up the trail. After about half an hour of climbing, we were starting to get a bit sweaty, when a beautiful waterfall appeared. The local climbed into the pool below, picked off some wild Aloe Vera and we got in as well. The water was bath warm, a hot spring but the waterfall was freezing cold. We walked back down and passed a wooden shack at the bottom. Two Rastas were putting dried marijuana through a mincing machine. - 'Want to but some smoke?' Uttered one of the Rastas through his dreadlocks. We tried a puff and in a few minutes, we were both so stoned that giggling was about all of the speech we could manage. We bought a small bag of the stuff and headed back to the bus stop.

For the next few days, I spent my time in Rodney Bay. Rob had gone completely native, living on a beach, living off the land; mangoes, breadfruit coconut and fish but that was too much for me and I stayed on Voyager. By now I was close to broke. The bank account was running dry and I knew soon I would have to go back to England. Mike came back and told me that the owner wanted Voyager to be delivered to Grenada. He had no budget to pay me but there was food and beer on board. I wanted to see the Caribbean and here was my chance, Mike had decided to stop at loads of islands on the way. The owner, Anthony Brown arrived and we were off south.

One of the first places we visited was the small island of Bequia, in those days there was no airport, you could only get there by boat and it was seen as something of a hippy hang out. Ashore there was a big vegetable market and it was there that we met The Mighty Skyscraper, who was one of the nicest men you should ever wish to meet. The nickname came from a song contest that he had won, and was rightly proud of. Although we did not know him from Adam, he invited us to his house to have dinner. Boney fish, pumpkin and sweet potato was beautifully cooked by his wife, served on the kind of plastic plates you take camping. The house was modest to say the least but it was extremely tidy and clean. After dinner, Skyscraper poured some Jack Iron rum from a barrel, which literally blew your head off. You had to slam it down as otherwise it just evaporated into the roof of your mouth and up to your brain. He produced a guitar and played ska music. In the early 80s I had listened to the British version of Ska Music from bands like Madness, Buster Blood Vessel, The Beat and The Specials. Here was Skyscraper showing where the music of my younger generation had come from. It was a memorable evening, I am sure the Mighty Skyscraper has since gone to the great gig in the sky, but thank you man.

We sailed through and stopped at many of the Windward Islands; Mustique, Petit St.Vincent and many more. The owner insisted on cooking the daily dinner and having downed more than his fair share of Sugar Cane Brandy, the dinner often ended up on the galley floor before it was served on a plate but we didn't care. I had labelled the St.Lucian marijuana 'special oregano" and put it in the spice rack. I think the owner put it in every meal.

Eventually we arrived in Grenada and I flew back to England the next day. I remember the plane was eight hours late because of a blocked toilet, the passengers were incensed. Me, I had taken 23 days to cross the Atlantic by sail, eight hours was nothing.

Chapter 6

Eats Shoots and Leaves

Back in England, the property market was still screwed and having resisted the temptation for many years, I finally joined the family business. It paid the bills and on top of that I had the opportunity to take time off to go yacht racing. I can't remember how but I joined the Giant Panda crew. The Hugh Welbourne Two Tonner was built for the 1983 Admiral's Cup but didn't win the trials. I raced on Giant Panda in La Nioularge 1989. She was owned by Nick Morrell, Managing Director of The Guardian Newspaper, and an architect called Peter Porter, who lived in Esher and funnily enough was the previous owner of the first house that I bought. I still have a Giant Panda crew shirt at home which is white, if you see a blue one on a chick that meant she had been pandarized by one of the crew. The crew's motto was in latin around the badge: Manducare et Virga Relinquo (eats, shoots and leaves). Giant Panda was soon retired after I joined the crew, but the owners introduced me to Terry and Sue Robinson, who had just bought a second hand S&S Swan 42 called Assuage. I raced for the Robinsons for over ten years.

In the early days of Assuage, we raced in the Lymington Spring and Winter Series and RORC Offshores with some success. In 1990, we went to Cork Week for the first time and it was fantastic. It was not a huge regatta, maybe 150 boats, but what a laugh. We also attended the Swan Europeans in Guernsey and like Cork Week, there was a corinthian spirit. Racing was very competitive but there were few professionals then, and not allowed at all at Cork Week. It was about winning but it was just as important to have a good time. Terry and Sue raced with their daughters, and their youngest Phillippa really took to it, and in hindsight, that it what really spurred Terry and Sue on. I was just a grinder, I learnt loads, but it was a hobby, not a career. I remember the first offshore with Assuage. Terry asked for our passports to fill out the crew form and saw that I was born in Baghdad, Iraq. "I'm not putting that on the declaration! We will all get arrested when we get to France!" laughed Terry. He put Bagshott as my place of birth, much to everybody's amusement.

In 1994, Assuage returned to Cork Week, it was also my stag week. To say, we had a few drinks would be the understatement of the millenium. We shut the beer tent every night. One particular evening, was sponsored by Mount Gay Rum. Acky (who is now sailing with the Angels – God bless him), liberated a case of Mount Gay and we fully got on it. We returned to our humble abode, totally polluted. All save Mike Broughton, who had refrained from going out on the large. There were five of us sleeping in a bedroom, three on the floor, myself in the top bunk and Micky B on the bottom. I flung myself into the bunk and proceeded to snore like a freight train. Micky had enough; raised his feet and projected me out of the bunk, onto the three guys below. The politest way to explainwhat happened next, was that the impact forced me to lose control of my lower intestine. The lads on the floor were not amused at the crushing blow, and the realisation that there was an after effect. I crawled to the bathroom, but was unable to find the light switch. Fumbling in the dark, I sat on what I thought was the bog, and finished what I had started.

Assuage Boat Captain was John Giblet, the saltiest sea dog I have ever met. John was in his late 60s but a life at sea, including the first Whitbread, had fashioned him into a proper seamen. After racing the following day, John waited until the Robinsons had left the boat and after we had finished the wash down, we were called into a huddle. "Lads, someone coiled one down in the bath last night." hissed John. "Don't worry, I cleaned it up, but please remember we have ladies in the house. Now on yer way!"

That Christmas, we all gathered at the Robinsons for the traditional end of year party. Terry and Sue gave us all the same present each year; a bone china coffee mug with the seasons results printed on it. Except that year, the only word written on my mug was Coiler – the nickname stuck, so to speak.

It was about this time that a new method of communicating became available, it was called the World Wide Web. In those early days, a dial up connection of 64k, and a bunch of yanks talking gobble-de-gook in forums, was the main action. It was not exactly ground breaking for me, but it was fun talking to someone in California from the back of a dry cleaners. Producing a web site in those days required an understanding of basic computer codes like C+. Languages like HTML were in their infancy. Today there are over a billion websites, in 2000 there were just 17 million. Yahoo Groups was started in the late 90s. This allowed a crude, yet free and easy, platform to invite people to join a group and read about the posts, effectively a blog. I created a group called Bang the Corner, and posted about yacht racing regattas, and some of the cool boats being raced. It got to about 500 people, mainly discussing who was shagging who at regattas.

In 1996, Terry and Sue Robinson launched a new Swan 48, still called Assuage, but this was a new Frers design and sailed properly, she was a real weapon at the time. We had the nucleus of the crew and that was enhanced with some top professionals. Sailmakers Tom McWilliam and John Brinkers, were regular crew and supplied hi-tech sails. We started winning, inshore and offshore, a real game changer for the team. The crew started to evolve and in came Mike Broughton as regular navigator. Mike was in the Royal Navy, and could bring along a lot of guys from the services. One of them was a Royal Marine, with a back like a dining table, Dom Mee. - My life was to change!

Swan 48 Assuage was very successful, winning the Swan Europeans and numerous RORC offshores. Terry became Commodore of the RORC and introduced IRC and IRM during his tenure.
I was an amateur, and in racing terms, I always have been, but I was hooked. I was living, breathing and talking yacht racing, but there was no way I could go professional. I was just a grinder and there was now way I could support my family, just doing that.

Terry and Sue decided to take Assuage to the Med. By then I had been hitting the gym pretty hard, I had trimmed down to 85 kilos and was sharing the grinding with Dom, who introduced me to the GU. The Grinders Union code was fairly basic: 1. Don't touch leather. 2. Don't touch small ropes. 3. Watch out for the ouchy thing (boom). 4. Don't trust trimmers.

The first day of the Copa Del Rey in Palma Mallorca, we saw 20 knots, and trying to grind in a 149% overlapping headsail made from cuben fibre, was not for the weak or faint hearted. Racing under IMS, we were never going to be competitive for the regatta, but this was a warm up for the Swan Worlds. We did manage to bang a corner one race, and take a bullet, beating a team led by Russell Coutts – one for the scrap book!

"Hey Coiler! Do you want to talk me through that 4th tack on the second downwind leg?" commented Dom Mee, with menace in his tone. "Oh yeah, it wasn't all the way in, but Tom had told me to get my weight up, and he would finish it off." came my honest reply. "You handed over a grind to a trimmer!?" accused Dom.

Despite a weak protest, I admitted my crime and after consulting with the Chairman of the GU, by telephone, punishment was meated out. "Tomorrow, you will be grinding both sides.. all day." Fortunately Day Two was a bit lighter, and I served my sentence, although I was bleeding through my eyes by the end of it.

The next regatta was the Swan Worlds in Sardinia. Over 100 Swans were up for it and Assuage was racing with two other well sailed Swan 48s. An Aussie team called Loki, and another British boat, Broadsword. It blew 30 knots plus all week and we had an epic regatta. The Assuage team had been together for a number of years, and our boat handling in big breeze was top banana. However, Loki, which had a Jib Top advantage, pipped up by half a point. We swapped crew shirts with them after the last race... real appreciation of a fantastic competition in amazing conditions.

There was a GU meeting during the regatta, the night before lay day. We had agreed to meet in a back street bar after racing, and about 20 huge guys turned up. At 5'6" on tip toes, I was by far the smallest grinder there, most of the crowd were well over 6ft tall and heavily built. We had a 50 euro ahead kitty, which I was trusted with. Now 20 huge blokes, in a swanky Sardinian bar, sort of stand out, and it wasn't long before a waiter came over and arrogantly flicked his head at me, since I was holding a large sum of money. "Forty beers, I said in my best bar Italian." The waiter shrugged his shoulders, to say he didn't understand, so a flashed him ten fingers, four times. The beers started to arrive and once delivered he asked me for the money. I said..we pay later, and suddenly his English became perfect. "No you pay now!" he shouted.

20 big blokes started staring at him and he began to shrink. "I said no, we pay when we leave, and can we please have 40 more beers and some crisps and nibbles and stuff." After spending a fortune, and a few hours discussing grinding techniques, and the fittest women on the planet, we paid the bill and went our separate ways.

After racing with Terry and Sue Robinson for about ten years, they retired from yacht racing. Reading between the lines, Assuage had run its course. To go bigger or better would require a huge investment and a change of personnel to professional. It wasn't what they wanted and Phillippa Robinson, got engaged, which was the finale.

Terry, Sue – Thank you from the bottom of my heart.

Chapter 7

The Grandaddy of the Caribbean

With the Assuage programme all wrapped up, a few of the crew, Mike Broughton, Andrew and Jane Mc Lelland, Dom Mee, Ian Finlay and myself, started sailing on another Swan 48; Murka, owned by Misha Mouratov and half the crew were Russian and spoke very little English. Russians often get tarred with a bad brand, arrogance and selfishness, but I can assure you Misha and his merry men are some of the most warm-hearted and considerate people you could ever meet. Misha decided to race in the Caribbean, and with the chance of returning to the best place on the planet to sail, after a ten year sabbatical, I jumped at the chance.

Piggy (God rest his soul) picked a bunch of us up from Antigua airport in a big old American car and handed out the beers, including one for himself, even though he was driving. We pulled up next to a Police car at some traffic lights and Piggy said cheers to officers, bottle in hand, which they acknowledged. ' What's the rule on drinking and driving in Antigua?' I asked. "Oh a beer is okay, but you wouldn't do that with a rum and coke.' replied Piggy.

Slava was one of the Russian crew, a lovely guy, full of fun and a top trimmer. Due to the language barrier, most of the communication on board was via hand signals, but we decided that with a kite sheet in his hands, this was difficult for Slava. He didn't speak a single word of English, so we decided to teach him four important words – Trim, Stop, Rum & Coke.

There was a bit of a cock up with the accommodation, and myself, Finlay and Dom ended up staying in a shack in Marsh Village. Today a lot of boat bums stay there but back then it was very local. We had nothing in the house, save bottles of beer in the fridge. After racing each day, we went there for a siesta, and the next door neighbours provided the afternoon cabaret. The father of the house would return home from work, and his missus would give it to him good, on the doorstep. Cursing and swearing at him in the local dialect. You couldn't understand much of what she said, but you could tell she wasn't impressed, as she wailed at him, sucking her teeth, marching around him and waving her arms like a dervish. Friday night he didn't come home as usual. We were discussing what might have happened? Had he found another woman? Fled to another island? Sought sanctuary in the local church? We came home late evening to see his car rammed into the hedge next to the house..he had obviously driven home worse for wear, he must have really got it that night!

Antigua Sailing Week was, and still is, an amazing event, with some incredible boats, back in 2005 we won the Racer/Cruiser Class on Murka. The early Transpac 52 Rosebud and Esmeralda, two duelling canting keel Z-86s, Hasno Platner's Morning Glory and Roy Disney's Pyewacket, and the enormous Mari Cha IV and Peter Harrison's Sojana. The conditions were as amazing as the boats. 15-20 knots, two metre seas, 25 degrees in the water and the air; I had died an gone to heaven. I wanted more of it, and managed to get back to Antigua racing on Adrian Lee's Cookson 50, Lee Overlay Partners. The chance was open for me to work as a journalist in the Caribbean, I took it with both hands.

Chapter 8

Exabitten

It's amazing who you meet, and what you learn, over a dry cleaning counter, I often joke that becoming a yacht racing journalist, after running a dry cleaning business, was a natural progression. However, when you talk to joe public, you learn how to listen, and how to push the buttons to get a good story. I remember an old boy coming into the shop, he could hardly lift his head off his chest, he must have been in his 90s. He presented a tie for dry cleaning, which was embroidered with an elephant with a knot tied in its trunk and the letters C.R.A.F.T. I asked him if it was a club tie. He replied; 'no it was a present from my son-in-law.' - 'Oh really what do the letters stand for?' - 'Can't remember a fucking thing.' Was his dry answer.

I knew Keith 'Irish' Groves from the Assuage days, he happened to use our Wimbledon dry cleaners and introduced me to Steve White aka AB (Aussie Bastard). AB worked for Shaun Frohlich in the IT industry, and 'Fro also owned an IMX 40, Exabyte 2. Off I trundled to Dartmouth Regatta, for the first sail with Fro, which carried on for a good six years and three boats. The Exabyte 2 crew was a bit of a mix of abilities but we all had one thing in common. We were hell bent on enjoying everything Dartmouth had to offer. If you haven't done the regatta, you should do. Set over the last bank holiday of the summer in the West Country, the whole town is alive, including a full on fun fare. First day, we went out on the water and smashed out a win. Fro was ecstatic, and insisted that we would be going straight out on the lash, as soon as we hit the dock. We all met in the nearest pub, but there was no sign of Fro? We got a ten quid whip together and headed for the bar but before we could order, Fro arrived and said he would get them in. He returned with seven halves of cider and an empty pint glass, and proceeded to empty an inch out of each one into the bigger glass. Where upon, he produced a small bottle of sloe gin and topped up the drinks, pouring the remainder into the pint glass. 'Right lads-down in one, and the last to finish does the pint.' Well needless to say, the blue touch paper was fully lit.

We became a very close knit team on Exabyte 2, led by Fro, who has the amazing ability to galvanise a team into a formidable fighting unit. We won numerous regattas including winning the IRC Nationals Overall and we were the top British boat for the 2002 Rolex Commodores' Cup. Fro sold E2 and replaced it with the IMX45 Exabyte 3. The team had an amazing run of wins offshore, winning trophy after trophy. However, the team remained amateur and we still had a real laugh on board – Great times. After Exabyte 3 came the Farr 45, Exabyte 4. We had 8 boats one design racing in the Solent, which was incredibly good fun. The stand out day for me was racing in The Solent one windy afternoon. The fleet were just about to go into a start sequence, when we were told the two Volvo Ocean Race teams had just entered the Solent, finishing the Transatlantic leg from Annapolis. We postponed racing and got the fog horns out, and gave Team Ericsson, one hell of a welcome. We got back into the starting sequence, just as Pirates of the Caribbean came into view. Ian 'Budgie' Budgen was driving, as this was home waters for him. Pirates of the Caribbean crossed the Farr 45 fleet upwind on starboard, it was blowing 30 knots, and we were all on the edge of control. Later Budgie told me that Pirates' skipper, Paul Cayard, said – 'who the hell are these nutters?'

Exabyte 4 racing in the Farr 45 Fleet

In 2004, Exabyte 4 went to Cork Week. I was returning ten years after my stag week, and I had visions of little Louays running around Crosshaven. We stayed in Curly's house, which was a three story town house near the best boozer in town, Cronin's. Curly showed us round the house, with his cigarette ash falling on his carpet. 'Here's the bar, I want you to drink it all.' said Curly pointing at a well over 100 cans of beer stacked from floor to ceiling. 'The hi-fi is over there, crank it up the whole way, and keep it going all night and have the biggest party in the town, invite everybody.'

By now my snoring had become legendary, and I was given a tent in the garden, which the lads used to throw full cans of beer at, while I was in it! As instructed, we had a huge party on the last night, over 100 people on the lash. Curly turned up and introduced us to iron board surfing. Crashing down the stairs on an ironing board, smashing into the retaining wall.

Fro married his lovely wife Emily, and decided to get stuck into Etchells one-design, winning the National and European Championships. Fro and Emily are still very much close friends, and Fro has supported me in more ways than one, especially through maters of the heart and business over the years!

Chapter 9
Complaint to Cape Town

Bangthecorner.com started to grow in popularity, I was starting to get a good following, which led to the first paid work for journalism. I had my first break some years before, writing up the daily reports for the Royal Ocean Racing Club, especially the Easter Challenge and the IRC Nationals. All thanks to Janet Grosvenor, who taught me all about Oxford commas. However, my spelling and grammar are still pants!

Steve Hayles was just about to go on his third round the world race, and we had become good friends. He suggested that I write a serious article for bangthecorner, and he was willing to spill the beans on the Volvo Ocean Race. Now remember, back in those days, the vast majority of yacht race reporting was of the blue blazer variety. Steve proceeded to tell me about how when the crew on Dolphin & Youth finished their first Southern Ocean leg in 1994, they were thrown out of their own welcome party for poor behaviour. Steve was only 20 at the time, and still is the youngest navigator to take part in the race. They left the party without too much of a commotion, but then decided to ride on the roof of their transit van through Auckland, sort of open-top-bus stylie.

Well when the feature got published, I got an email from the Volvo Ocean Race CEO, Glenn Bourke, complaining that the story was to one-sided. I asked him if he would like to give the other side and he agreed to an interview. I was expecting a frosty reception when I turned up at VOR HQ, but instead I was given a tour of the building and allowed to sit in on a private meeting. The VOR was just about to go canting keel, with the first generation VO70s. It was an incredible insight into an uber development in the race. One lasting memory was Mike 'Moose' Sanderson, who went onto skipper the winner ABN AMRO 1. I was leaving at the same time as Moose, and I couldn't believe the heap of a car he was driving. A battered-up old hatchback. Moose now runs Doyle Sails and I doubt if he is still running that car anymore! Glenn Bourke introduced me to Lizzie Green (Ward), and I started writing articles about the race, one was about how the weather information is transmitted to the boats, and I entered the world of satellite communication.

ABN AMRO ONE (Volvo Ocean Race)

In the 2001-02 edition of the VOR, it was reported that teams were spending huge amounts of time and money downloading all sorts of weather information. This was a major advantage to the well-funded teams. For the 2005-06 edition the teams could only get weather info from VOR HQ, via an ftp link. INMARSAT were brought in as race sponsor, providing the air time, for weather info, yacht telemetry, and media back from the boats. Glenn Bourke recommended me as a travelling reporter and I ended up in Cape Town a week later! Maritime satellite communication was going through a huge change at the time. The previous service FLEET was being replaced by BGAN, and with it the data transmission rate was going through the roof, allowing video to be sent back from the boats in HD. The service was so new they hadn't launched the satellite over the Pacific, so the boats were equipped with two domes, the new FB500 and a Fleet

33 for the Pacific. At the time, INMARSAT were working closely with the satellite dome manufacturer, Thrane & Thrane. In Cape Town, I met Jens Ewerling and Morten Dysseholm, from Thrane & Thrane. They had a stand showing the new dome. Jens had done a lot of racing, including the Admiral's Cup, but neither new the sailors very well. They asked me if I could get some sailors to the stand. I returned with Stan Honey, and a TV crew that I was working with for Boatson.TV, they nearly fell off their chairs, as Stan Honey went on record, stating that it was the best piece of kit he had ever used!

Thrane & Thrane were so impressed with me, they asked me to work for them for the next leg. For the 2005-06 race, the route was the traditional one, and after Cape Town, the fleet raced to Melbourne Australia. I returned to the UK for a few weeks work at the dry cleaners, and then got ready to pack my bags for Australia.

On the first leg of the VOR 2005-06, the vulnerability of the new canting keel boats was all too apparent, Pirates of the Caribbean and Movistar retired from the leg on the first night, after shipping in tons of water through the 'fish tank' around the canting keel, and through a cracked hull respectively. The second leg from Cape Town to Melbourne gave the fleet their first taste of the Southern Ocean, I knew a fair few of the sailors as friends, and I was praying for them.

Chapter 10
Title

Down Under

I was starting to spend a lot of time away from the dry cleaning business, but I couldn't tell the staff what I was up to. Travelling around the world to follow a yacht race was an alien concept to them. When I got to Melbourne following the race, my phone went at about 4 a.m. "Are you abroad Louay?" enquired the manageress of the Wimbledon Branch. "Yes, just popped over to France with the kids." was my dishonest reply. "Look can you tell the factory to send me a big pack of carrier bags, I have asked three times." - "Okay no problem, I will do it now." It dawned on me that I couldn't carry on with this alternative lifestyle. I would have to make a choice, and I have never regretted kicking dry cleaning into touch!

I have done a fair bit of travelling but this was my first trip to Oz. London to Hong Kong was the first leg, and 12 hours in cattle class, did not endear me to doing the same to Melbourne. After stumbling around HK airport in a daze, I got in the queue with the rest of the livestock to board the next flight. There is often a group of guys checking out the passengers on long haul flights. Usually they are looking for someone who has been flagged up for a dodgy passport or visa. So when the suits were hanging around check-in, I didn't think they were after me. My passport and work permit were all in order, but it was me they were after. It was all down to the Muhammad cartoons crisis

A Danish journalist had published some cartoons depicting the muslim prophet Muhammad. The issue eventually led to protests around the world, including violent demonstrations and riots in some Muslim countries. The Danish Prime Minister at the time described the situation as, Denmark's worst international relations incident, since the Second World War.

Thrane & Thrane was a Danish company, and here I was, a

journalist with an Arab name, and a Danish work permit heading to Australia for just seven days. The guy in the tailor made suit was the Australian High Commissioner for Hong Kong. His henchman led me to a side room, and started to ask me questions. I explained that I was a yachting journalist, covering the Volvo Ocean Race. After consulting google, and putting me through a series of questions about the race more difficult that the final round of Mastermind. They decided I was telling the truth, and bid me on my way. I asked for an escort back to the front of the check-in, and they obliged.

"Thanks heavens that's all sorted out," I said to the check-in girl. "How on earth did I end up in economy!" I uttered in astonishment-lying through my teeth. "You are in economy." replied the check-in girl. "Oh you must be joking! Do you want me to get the High Commissioner back again?!" - British Airways; Thanks for the upgrade!

Melbourne is an interesting city, sort of like Guildford on steroids, with a river running through its heart and leafy suburbs. However, I didn't get to see a lot of it. I would love to return but to this date I have never been back to Australia. I was booked into the swankiest hotel in Melbourne, The Crown Plaza, and unable to sleep. I headed for breakfast as soon as it opened, and their was one resident, and I recognised straight away.

Mark Taylor was the opening batsman for the Australian cricket team for seven Ashes series wins in a row. From 1989 to 2003 Australia were an invincible outfit. But worse than that, he was the guy that blew away a massive winning bet for some impoverished students, and he needed to show his remorse!

I went to watch the Ashes in 1989 with some mates from Ealing College. Taylor and Marsh were opening, and destroyed the England bowling attack, never hitting the ball above knee height all day, smashing boundary after boundary. At the break for tea, with 2 hours remaining, we decided to have a silly bet with the on-site bookmaker. We bet that the pair would not be out and score another 100-120 runs by the close of pay. The odds were 30-1. We clubbed together £50, if it came in £1500 was the equivalent of 6 months grant at university. Things were going to plan, and we were starting to really enjoy the Ozzie dominance, then it all came crashing down. Derek Pringle bowled the last over, and Marsh smashed him all over the park, putting the run total above 120, and with it we tore up the betting slip.

In the Crown Plaza breakfast room, I told the story to Mark Taylor. He just shrugged and sipped his coffee.

Chapter 11
The Domster

Everyone is born with a fire inside them, it's like a pilot light in a boiler, in its normal state it is just flickering, and for most people it just stays that way. But some people ignite the flame with propellant, and Dom Mee knows how to turn on the gas.

I met Dom racing on Assuage, and we hit it off straight away. In 2001, Dom joined fellow Royal Marine, Tim Welford, in a bid to row across the North Pacific. They rowed for 138 days before being run down by a fishing trawler. I followed their progress every morning and then went to the gym, and did 2000 metres on a ergo-rower out of respect and admiration.

In his next adventure, Dom attempted to kayak the North West Passage. He befriended what seemed the entire Inuit Nation, and got attacked by a Musk Ox, but the expedition hit a wall of ice and Dom had no way through it. I asked Dom what he had learnt from the experience. He said that when you shoot an angry charging Musk Ox with a shot gun, it still hits you bloody hard, and doesn't die. Dom got the headlines for that, but his next big adventure resulted in numerous appearances on chat shows, all over the world.

*Dom Mee with Little Murka in St.John's New Foundland, Canada.
(www.dommee.co.uk)*

In 2005, Dom decided to do something really crazy. He modified a bosun dinghy with a survival interior, and decided to sail the 14ft Little Murka across the Atlantic, west to east, using only kites for propulsion, and totally unsupported. Dom invited me along to Canada as press officer, and we were joined by two of Dom's mates from the Royal Marines; Titch and Barry.

We nearly came off the plane in hand cuffs, after a bit of a drinking spree, which involved the duty free Vodka, and to be honest, we were in a right old state when we arrived in St John's, Newfoundland.

We found our digs and headed into town, stopping at the first bar we came to. Inside there wasn't a soul, save an old boy playing guitar, and his old lady behind the bar. We ordered up a round of beers, and Barry, who had demolished most of the in-flight vodka, decided he was going to dance. After crashing into several tables and chairs, he slalomed into the gents, and didn't reappear for some minutes.

Titch went to check on him and returned with Barry slumped over his shoulder. Titch gestured a chopping sign to his neck, and uttered the word- extraction, taking Barry back to the digs. We returned to the same bar the following evening, and Barry was asking what we were doing in a shit-hole. "We were in here last night, they are nice people." commented Titch. "Bullshit!" responded Barry. "I bet you a tenner I have never been in here before." The old lady appeared at the bar, and shouted to her old man. "George, the drunkest man in the world's back."

The run ashore to St.John's was a full-on pants wetting laugh. With the three Bootnecks (slang for Royal Marines), breaking all the rules. One night they managed to clear a big queue at a hot dog stand, with a counter terrorism manoeuvre. "You with the ketchup! Move away from the hot dog vendor!"

Little Murka arrived in a container and we went down to the docks to do the logistics of getting her ready for the Atlantic. St. John's was once a thriving cod fishing port, populated by people of Irish descent, who had fished from New Foundland since the 17th century. It was weird to hear everybody talking in an Irish accent, thousands of miles from their original home. Modern day St.John's was no longer making a fortune from cod, huge Chinese factory fishing boats had destroyed St.John's fishing industry, and the docks were close to desolate.

An old man was asked to break the seal on Little Murka's container. He was no more than 5ft tall, had an elf-like beard, and the turn-ups on his filthy trousers, that went up to his knees. I swear he would have got a part in the Wizard of Oz. He was smoking a roll-up and took a couple of big puffs and lit an acetylene torch with the cherry, cutting through the container seal. Like some weird version of Yoda, he cackled off and we opened the doors.

Little Murka had survived the containerised Atlantic crossing, but we needed a few things. We made a list and headed off to the chandlery. "Have you got a fender?" Sure came the reply, and a fender the size of a bath tub was brought out. "Anything smaller?" Nope was followed by a series of nopes from anything smaller than a shopping trolly on our list. We headed out of town to Canadian Tyre, where you could buy anything from biltong to a fully automatic hunting rifle, and the problems were solved.

Dom decided to set off in Little Murka, even though the weather outlook was looking very bad. There was no stopping him. After several weeks at sea, he had made little progress, and was still on the Grand Banks, 300 miles offshore, in the location for the film, The Perfect Storm, and by God, did he find one.

Hurricane Rita was the fourth-most intense Atlantic hurricane ever recorded and the most intense tropical cyclone ever observed in the Gulf of Mexico. Part of the record-breaking 2005 Atlantic hurricane season, which included three of the six most intense Atlantic hurricanes ever recorded (along with Wilma and Katrina), Rita was the seventeenth named storm, tenth hurricane, and fifth major hurricane of the 2005 season.

Dom was riding out the hurricane shut inside the survival pod with a sea anchor preventing the little boat from being tossed from wave to wave. Little Murka was being rolled and rolled but the design held firm, and she kept self righting, that was until the water containers in the cockpit were thrown outside the hull still attached to their lanyards. The additional weight outside the lifelines meant that she didn't self-right, the sea anchor snapped, and water was pouring into he upturned pod. Dom knew he had to get out, and already in his survival suit, drank the miniature bottle of whisky he had been saving for his birthday.

He clambered onto the outside of the hull, with a waterproof video camera. I have seen the footage and it is by far the most harrowing video I have ever seen. The waves were monumental, and Dom was clinging to the up turned hull. Death was staring him in the face until he got lucky.

A monster of a wave hit Little Murka, and the force put the boat back up right. Dom climbed back into the soaked interior, sloshing around checking to see if he had any power. At that point the Royal Marine Commando, who had served in Northern Island, Iraq, Bosnia, and other god-for-saken hell holes, fully broke down, on camera. He hit the EPIRB distress beacon, and for the once and only time in his crazy life, he called for help. The Canadian Coastguard picked him up days later.

Little Murka washed up on a beach in Ireland months later, covered in barnacles. The boat had made it across the Atlantic, Dom hadn't but he was alive to tell the tale. My old mate went into the private security business after that, employing hundreds of ex-bootnecks as armed guards in the Indian Ocean. Honestly I could write a book about the man.. he has written one himself. Kiting the Hurricane – read it.

Dom Mee aka Cruella de Vil. I am the Dalmatian on the right. Titch far left. This was taken on a crazy New Year's Eve in Exmouth, Devon. Home of the Royal Marines.

Chapter 12

Cold Grey Ocean Night

Louay Habib @ Thu May 18 09:46:00 BST 2006

Cold grey ocean night, frozen steel and dancing light.\|
Look out on a barren sky with eyes that know the darkness in the waves.\|
Shadows in the mist, dreams of friends and flower fields.\|
Catch the breeze and the winter seas, in colours in the foaming screaming waves.\|
\|
I hope you understand why they go to sea.\|
How they suffer for their sanity. How they try to set their spirit free.\|
They would not listen, they do not know how, but will they listen now?\|
\|
Cold grey ocean night, flaming stars that brightly blaze.\|
Swirling clouds in violet haze, reflect in waves of white and blue.Colours changing hue.

Morning tinge of pink champagne.\|
Weathered faces lined in pain are soothed beneath Neptune's loving hand.\|
\|
For they could not know it, but still the dream was true.\|
And when the storm did rage, on that desolate night.\|
They risked their lives, as sailors often do.

\|
No one could have stopped them, it is what they have to do.\|
And if it takes them, then at least they have been true.\|
\|
Cold grey ocean night, a wondrous room with waves for walls.\|
Unbound heads amidst waterfalls with eyes that watch the real world and can't forget.\|
The stranger that he's met.\|
\|
He's a ragged man in reeking clothes with a red raw face and a bloody nose

With a gallant stance at the crowded dock.\|
\|
Try to think what this says to you.\|
Are they mad or is it you?\|
Have you tried to set yourself free?\|
Perhaps you never will.\|
\|
Copyright-Louay Habib in Memory of Hans Horrevoets (with thanks to Don McLean).

Printed in Great Britain
by Amazon